MW00509634

Impact on NFTs on the Environment

How, and Where to Buy, Sell or Create Your Own

NFT: All Current Possibilities.

Hollie C Hargreaves

Copyright 2022. All Rights Reserved.

This document provides exact and reliable information regarding the topic and issues covered. The publication is sold with the idea that the publisher is not required to render accounting, officially permitted, or otherwise qualified services. If advice is necessary, legal or professional, a practiced individual in the profession should be ordered.

From a Declaration of Principles which was accepted and approved equally by a Committee of the American Bar Association and a Committee of Publishers and Associations.

In no way is it legal to reproduce, duplicate, or transmit any part of this document in either electronic means or printed format. Recording of this publication is strictly prohibited, and any storage of this document is not allowed unless with written permission from the publisher. All rights reserved.

The information provided herein is stated to be truthful and consistent. Any liability, in terms of inattention or otherwise, by any usage or abuse of any policies, processes, or Instructions contained within is the solitary and utter responsibility of the recipient reader. Under no circumstances will any legal obligation or blame be held against the publisher for reparation, damages, or monetary loss due to the information herein, either directly or indirectly.

Respective authors own all copyrights not held by the publisher.

The information herein is offered for informational purposes solely and is universal as such. The presentation of the data is without a contract or any guarantee assurance.

Sommario

Chapter 1:   How, and Where to Buy, Sell or Create Your Own NFT?

Before we can buy or create an NFT, we must first address one question: How do we determine which NFT to buy? Elegance, emotional depth, and social worth are only a few of the subjective reasons for acquiring an NFT. Scarcity, as with other valuable commodities, is an essential consideration.

We'll be looking at rarity if we use the Pokémon example for trading cards. Each Pokémon card indicates the number of cards in its collection as well as the rarity levels.

Likewise, each NFT has a finite quantity as well as unique characteristics, often known as metadata. Not all pieces are created equal, and some will be more scarce than others, particularly if a specific quality is greatly desired. As a result, one important component in determining the value of

NFTs is their metadata, which is the origin of the piece's attributes, such as the name, picture, or video connected with it.

Most ERC-721 tokens provide a defined set of information that may be used to show the name, description, and picture of a digital asset. The information and accompanying files are released onto the InterPlanetary File System (IPFS) as part of the minting process.

IPFS enables us to hold asset metadata in a safe, accessible, decentralized, and public manner. NFT information is often frozen to guarantee that your NFTs may be proudly shown for years to come. This implies that the NFT's properties will be permanently secured and saved using the decentralized file storage system, and they will be impossible to change or remove.

The information for NFTs that may be utilized

as functioning game pieces can also be left unfrozen and then used to show dynamic abilities and statistics. In this situation, the NFT information may be altered or evolved in-game, revealing new features. In certain situations, it enhances their uniqueness—imagine mixing various pieces to make a new, distinct NFT character! All of this is made feasible by utilizing the token's information.

You may examine an NFT's metadata directly on the smart contract or on an NFT marketplace like OpenSea, which extracts the smart contract data. The latter way, which is more intuitive and as easy as picking on an NFT in the market and checking its attributes, is used by the majority of consumers.

Why would somebody purchase a non-fungible token?

The more you attempt to understand the

strange and mystical world of NFTs, the more you may wonder why anyone would buy an NFT. There are a few motives why those with extra cash choose to invest.

Scarcity

There's nothing like a feeling of uniqueness to pique someone's interest in a certain item. Because NFTs have one and only owner, they generate a lot of scarcity. This motivates potential purchasers to get fixated on a certain item and fear that someone else will become an exclusive possessor of an NFT that they desire.

Consider when you see a pair of shoes you want to purchase and the website informs you that there is only one pair remaining. If you're like the majority of us, this elevates your feeling of scarcity and motivates you to make the purchase—even if it doesn't make economic sense for you.

Collectability

It can be said that NFTs represent trading cards for the wealthy. A lot of people also compare it to trading baseball cards activity in almost every school yard in America. These cards do not have intrinsic value. They only have the value that the market assigns.

The changing value on the other hand, is the one in charge, and the one that transforms their selling potential. Quite similar to high-risk gambling. This is how the process gets simple when it comes to parallels between the art world, and NFTs.

In difference, NFTs give artists a different chance, and more liberty because they are no longer reliant on galleries or traders to sell their work. The creators, or in this case artists, are able to sell their work to purchasers, and keep a lot of money to themselves.

So far, we've learned about the concept, the operation, and other critical components of NFTs. Most of you are probably wondering how we can make NFTs or buy/sell them. Let's talk about how we can make NFTs, purchase them, and trade them.

Creating an NFT

There are few possibilities for constructing NFTs (in terms of their blockchains), and Ethereum is the most efficient, if not the only, method to get engaged with NFTs.

When it comes to the various blockchains that support NFT activities, each type of blockchain has its own approach of dealing with NFTs. For example, if you use the Binance Smart Chain blockchain, you will only be able to interact with NFTs utilizing

Binance Smart Chain assets.

This implies you won't be able to manufacture, purchase, or trade NFTs from other blockchains on the Binance Smart Chain blockchain network. As a result, it is strongly advised that you utilize the Ethereum blockchain because it is the most widely used form of blockchain for dealing with NFTs.

To make your own NFTs using the Ethereum blockchain, you will need to have various prerequisites and demands.

You'd need an Ethereum wallet that supports the ERC-721 token standard. Some of the top Ethereum wallets on the market that follow the ERC-721 standard and deal with NFTs include MetaMask, Trust Wallet, and Coinbase Wallet.

A minimum Ether balance of $50 to $100 is required. Using wallets such as Coinbase Wallet, you may be able to purchase Ether using a variety of currencies like USD, GBP, and a variety of other fiat currencies.

However, if you choose a different type of wallet, you may need to purchase Ether through another cryptocurrency exchange. Following the acquisition of a wallet, you must focus on NFT platforms that will enable you to link your wallet to that platform and upload the digital asset that you wish to convert into an NFT.

We have previously examined the finest NFT markets on the market. Marketplaces are not only venues for buying and selling NFTs, but they also let you develop your own NFTs. You would, however, need to register with that marketplace and become an artist on their platform.

Some NFT markets, such as Rarible, OpenSea, and MIintable, offer a create button in the upper right corner of their site. So, for example, to better grasp the issue, imagine the medium of OpenSea.

A create button will take you to a screen that will ask you to connect with an Ethereum blockchain wallet. You will be instantly linked to the marketplace after entering your login and password. However, you may be requested to digitally sign a message in order to authenticate that the wallet data you have supplied are yours. There would be no fees or charges associated with this procedure of proving your ownership of your wallet.

The next step is to click the create button and then choose the "my collections" option. You will be able to see the create button after finishing this step. When you click that, a box will appear on the screen that will allow you to upload your artwork, give it a name, and create a description.

This procedure establishes a location where you may construct a folder to keep the NFTs you wish to make. You will be able to see a picture or any other asset that you have successfully added to your collection. After that, you may create a banner image by clicking on the pencil symbol in the upper right corner.

When this procedure is finished, you will be able to generate your first NFT. Now, click the "add new item" button, and you'll be prompted to sign another message. You will now be led to a window where you may submit the NFT picture, music, GIF, or other digital content.

Most systems, such as OpenSea, will give you possibilities to add some unique qualities and attributes to boost the rarity and uniqueness of the digital asset. There is also an option that allows users to enter information that no one else can access except the one who purchases them.

This material might include passwords or

other unique services that provide access to discount codes or contact information. After that, you must click "create," which requires a final signature to construct your NFT. Congratulations, your artwork has now been added to your collection.

The cost of creation — Some platforms, like Open Sea, will not charge a price to create an NFT; however, other marketplaces may. Most Ethereum-based markets would refer to this element as gas, which was previously addressed when discussing Ether.

This gas is the quantity necessary to carry out specific functions. While we're on the subject of producing NFTs, the gas would be required to manufacture NFTs on a marketplace. The costs of Ether would vary depending on the network and the exact sort of marketplace, and the fees may be significant.

A small tip from us: If you wish to do an Ether transaction, the charges may be significantly lower on weekends compared to weekdays. The major reason for this is the lower quantity of transactions that occur on weekends.

Selling NFTs

We now understand how to transform our digital assets into NFTs. Let's take a look at the process of selling those NFTs. To sell your NFTs, you must first locate them in your collection. After you've found them, you'll need to click on them and then select the "sell" option. When you pick the sell option, you will be sent to a price page where you may determine and define the terms of service of your transaction.

This includes the alternatives of holding an

auction for them or selling them for a fixed price.

Ether and some other types of ERC-20 tokens are among the cryptocurrencies that you may use to sell your NFTs. Nevertheless, most platforms would only accept transactions in their native currencies. For example, in the VIV3 marketplace, which runs on the FLOW blockchain's blockchain technology, the only cryptocurrency tokens with which you will be allowed to perform transactions are the FLOW tokens and only the FLOW tokens.

There is an edit option directly next to the collection in the OpenSea marketplace. By signing the message with your wallet and scrolling down a little, you'll find several options for royalties and the token you'd want to earn when selling your NFTs. As we all know, royalties have the potential to provide passive income for a lifetime whenever the underlying assets are sold. The royalty's procedure is effectively maintained with the assistance of smart contracts (thanks to Ethereum).

You may be charged a fee for listing your NFTs on a marketplace in some situations. As a result, while this is not true for all NFT marketplaces, it is preferable to deal with such scenarios.

Buying NFTs

Some aspects should be carefully considered before making a hasty purchase of NFTs. We will now be aware of these critical aspects, which are especially significant when acquiring NFTs.

The marketplace where you wish to buy NFTs.

The wallet you'll need in order to login to the site where the NFTs are offered.

The tokens (cryptocurrency) required to fund the wallet and purchase the NFTs.

It is about understanding whether the NFTs you wish to purchase are available at a specific time, such as through a pack or an art drop.

Popular Markets

OpenSea

Definitely, OpenSea is the leader, and it can be said that it will be on the throne for a while. OpenSea's platform hosts a wide range of digital materials, and it's completely free to sign up and explore the broad offers. It also helps artists and makers and includes a simple approach for creating your own NFT.

Because the marketplace accepts over 150 alternative payment tokens, the platform's name is suitable. OpenSea is a fine place to begin if you're new to the NFT world.

Axie Marketplace

Axie Marketplace is really representing Axie Infinity, a video game, as its online marketplace for NFTs. You have the supernatural beings here, known as Axies, that can be purchased, trained, and then pitted against the Axies of other players to gain points. With this marketplace, the users can buy new Axies, territories, and other in-game stuff.

These Axies can be created in the Ethereum network. As a result, they may be purchased and sold on a number of different NFT markets, as well as other cryptocurrency exchanges including Coinbase Global.

Larva Labs

Larva Labs is primarily known for the widely publicized CryptoPunks NFTproject. They were first distributed for free in 2017; however, some CryptoPunks have subsequently sold for millions of dollars. Larva Labs is also working on additional digital art pieces, such as Auto Glyphs, as well as Ethereum blockchain-based application development.

Larva Labs' punks are sold out. But this does not end here. Indeed, they can be bid on and purchased once again on multiple other marketplaces. It is important to mention that Larva Labs' tons of products, and plans are worth following, especially the one known as Meebits.

NBA Top Shot

NBA Top Shot is just the National Basketball Association's as well as Women's National Basketball Association's first step into the realm of NFT. Collectible moments like play highlights, video clips from games, and art from current, and previous basketball leagues.

The NBA made it as a marketplace that is closed by using the blockchain of Dapper Labs' Flow . If you want to sign up, and then purchase from the Top Shot marketplace website, do not worry. The process is quite simple. Believe it or not, collectibles here can be found for less than a dollar.

Rarible

Rarible is similar to OpenSea. An enormous marketplace that features every kind of NFT. This site allows you to sell, buy, or trade a lot of collectibles (including movies, music, art, etc.) Before you purchase, or sell something, you need to utilize the marketplace's own token Rarible, unlike OpenSea. The Ethereum blockchain serves as the foundation for Rarible.

The firm has formed alliances with a number of well-known corporations. Yum! Brands have featured art on Rarible, while cloud software behemoth Adobe has just joined with Rarible to properly protect the work of NFT artists and producers.

SuperRare

SuperRare, like Rarible, is creating a market for digital producers. The site features art, films, and 3D graphics, but collectors may pay using Ethereum.

SuperRare has announced the launch of its own coin, also called SuperRare, based on the Ethereum network. The tokens will be used to discover and choose young faces for the marketplace. SuperRare NFTs, like Rarible, may be bought and traded on OpenSea.

Foundation

Foundation Ethereum is used for sales. Since

its inception in early 2021, the market has sold more than $100 million in NFTs.

The Foundation community invites artists to the site, and purchasers just need a crypto wallet filled with Ethereum to begin making purchases. If you're seeking for a fast and simple way to start generating your own NFTs, Foundation might not be the greatest place to start, but the marketplace offers lots of artwork that can be seen in a simple style.

Nifty Gateway

This marketplace so far has given the biggest support of digital artists. Yes, we are talking about Beeple, and Grimes. This is an art supporting platform that exists thanks to the cryptocurrency known as Gemini. NFTs, often referred to as Nifties, are based on Ethereum.

You do not have a personal wallet here.

Instead of a personal one they are stored for you by Gemini and Nifty Gateway. While this may not be suitable for NFT collectors seeking greater flexibility in their art acquisitions, Nifty trades may also be conducted in fiat money (Euros, US dollars) without first purchasing cryptocurrency.

Mintable

Mintable, funded and created by Mark Cuban, a billionaire, wants to create a similar open marketplace to OpenSea. You will definitely need an Ethereum to engage in the purchasing and selling of NFTs on Mintable. The platform also allows creators of various sorts (from musicians to photographers) to mint NFTs in order to market their work as a digital asset.

An ambitious NFT creator or collector must first obtain an Ethereum from a cryptocurrency exchange, then link their wallet to Mintable to bid and buy on the marketplace.

Theta Drop

Our last, but not least, at the list is blockchain platform designed for the internet's decentralized transmission of video and television. Theta Drop, an NFT marketplace, made its first appearance in 2021 with digital memorabilia from the World Poker Tour. The first adopter of ThetaTV, which now streams videos.

Theta makes use of its own blockchain technology. To engage in the Theta Drop NFT market, you must first acquire Theta Token. Theta has the support of tons of crypto exchanges, including Binance, and the NFTs and tokens that someone gets or purchases, have the option to be saved as a cryptocurrency.

Is it a good time to buy NFTs?

The NFT boom has only recently begun, and from what we can see, it is likely to continue. In addition, numerous celebrities, like Shawn Mendez and Grimes (Elon Musk's child's mother), are using NFTs to sell digital goods like music or artwork. Based on this, NFTs would be more popular than what we are now witnessing. Furthermore, with more blockchains vying to provide NFT-related services, now is as good a moment as any to acquire NFTs.

NFTs as a form of investment

Even if there is considerable recognition of NFTs throughout the world, they are still regarded as a novel sort of investment.

Furthermore, determining the value of a digital asset is difficult, making NFTs a dangerous investment choice. When it comes to stocks, the likelihood of a price increase is greater, which means you will be able to sell it for a better price even after ten years, if not now. That is not the case with NFTs because they are artwork, and there is no guarantee that their price will rise.

You cannot predict whether the price of a meme, gif, or any other digital asset will rise. Regardless of what was written above, most of you would still consider NFTs to be a profitable kind of investing. If you do, make sure you set a budget for how much you will spend on them. Along with that, you should ensure that the risk tolerance of your investment portfolio is sufficient to deal with a loss caused by investing in NFTs (if any loss were to happen). Also, keep in mind that NFTs are very theoretical, which means you can't rely on them to get rich.

Even while NFTs are a fantastic type of

investment, they are not suitable for everybody, and not every digital asset is a great NFT. You might try your luck with NFTs if you have a large sum of money that you can afford to lose. If such is not the case, it is best to avoid becoming engaged with NFTs in order to keep your hard-earned money secure.

Before starting to engage in NFTs, creation, selling, and buying, keep the following in mind:

NFT investment is a personal decision, and choice. Of course, if you have some extra money at home that you do not need in the foreseeable future, do it, invest that money in NFT. Of course, this decision can be easier if the NFT you want to buy sparks a sentimental or emotional value to you.

Do not forget that NFTs and their value depend a lot on other people. To be more specific, their value is based on what someone else is ready to pay. With this in mind, the demand, or the amount of demand will always be the one that increases the price. Economic, technical, and fundamental features do not have meaning here at all.

If you plan to re-sell the NFT you have purchased, or if you created it and want to sell it, have in mind that it may sell for quite less than you expected it to. In a lot of cases people resold it for less than they bought it.

Always know that NFTs are quite close to capital gains taxes. Yes, in the same way people sell stocks. After all, they are highlighted as collectibles, and they may not gain preferential capital gains that are long-term. Of course, they may be taxed higher.

NFTs should be approached in the same way that people approach everything else. It is an investment just like every other investment that exists. The only thing new is the concept. Do your part – research, ask around, read books, and articles, and ultimately understand the risks that always come with NFTs.

NFT Scams to Avoid

Now that you're comfortable with the fundamentals of minting and trading NFTs, you're ready to dip your toes into the water and begin purchasing your very first NFT! But first, you must be informed of the potential hazards.

The following are a few frequent NFT scams to be aware of:

Fake Web Pages

One of the most common frauds is the imitation of NFT project websites or major markets such as OpenSea. Unwary individuals are frequently urged to connect their crypto wallets to the bogus website in order to mint or deal with an NFT. In most situations, the activity drains cash from users' wallets, while the more "lucky" ones find that they have been paying for a fake NFT.

So, how can you prevent being duped? Before you click on any online links, always double-check them. The official URLs are often posted in the restricted Discord channels (e.g., Announcement or FAQ channels) or on the project's Twitter page.

Another nice "mint habit" to develop is to read the comments on the project's social media platforms while you prepare for a mint. Scams are frequently identified by online sleuths, and if you spot any, take a step back and examine more. If you are skeptical but still want to buy or mint an NFT in the hopes of striking gold, connect using a fresh wallet with just the appropriate quantity of cash.

Always be cautious and conduct your own research!

Collections of Fake Items

If something appears to be too good to be true, it most likely is. The same is true for NFTs, so don't purchase that 1 ETH CryptoPunk just yet! Make certain that the NFT is part of the genuine collection and not a forgery.

Most high-profile collections will be marked with a "Verified Collection" badge on marketplaces like OpenSea. Some devious scammers try to imitate this by putting the confirmed tick in the bogus collection's logo.

If the "Verified Collection" tag is not accessible, it is essential to verify the official websites and community channels of the NFT collection to determine if the contract addresses match what you are purchasing.

Impersonation

Impersonation frauds have been around for a long time and, sadly, are still popular in the crypto realm. Scammers frequently imitate the project's customer support personnel in order to prey on unwary individuals in need of assistance. Typically, they are phishing efforts to get the targets' personal information and sensitive information, such as wallet seed phrases.

Fake giveaways are another prevalent fraud that fool and seduce users into linking their wallets to a bogus website or handing over their private keys. If the operation is successful, the users' cash will be at the mercy of the fraudsters, who will be able to drain all of the wallet's holdings.

Sophisticated hackers may even be able to circumvent protection and get access to the project's social media or Discord accounts. This effectively allows hackers to publish bogus "official links" in "official channels," fooling even the most cautious users, like in the example of Beeple's Discord group, which resulted in a user losing 38 ETH.

While there is no foolproof way to avoid such instances, you may do your homework by checking numerous sources (e.g., Twitter, Discord, Telegram, official website) before attempting to acquire or mint any NFTs.

As you become more involved in the Discord groups of various projects, you will begin to receive an increasing number of unprompted direct messages (DMs) or spam from other users. Avoid clicking on links provided by other users, since this is a strategy used by fraudsters to share phony websites in order to phish for private keys.

One approach to avoid this is to change the privacy settings in Discord to restrict direct messages from server members. You will filter out all private messages from users who are not on your friend list by doing so.

Lowball Offers

While not a scam, this is a common occurrence that both new and experienced NFT collectors should be aware of. Multiple offers for your NFT are frequent, especially for popular collections or unique pieces. When you receive an offer for your NFT, take particular attention to the coin denomination for the offer. Is the offer made in ETH, DAI, USDC, or another token?

Consider the following offer for Poet #3179. While 1.25 ETH may be a viable option for the NFT, 1.25 USDC is unquestionably not. In this situation, the bidder is hoping that the NFT owner accepts the offer by mistake in order to make a quick and simple profit, beware of these techniques!

As with many prosperous industries, there will always be unscrupulous actors looking to benefit from our mistakes in judgment. In general, with NFTs, the same traditional cybersecurity standards should be followed:

Never divulge the seed phrases in your wallet.

Verify and double-check the links you click on.

Cross-check and double-check information from numerous sources.

When connecting to suspicious websites, use a new wallet.

Conduct your own research at all times.

Chapter 2: NFT pitfalls and Strategies to Avoid Them

N on-fungible tokens (NFTs)—which might take the shape of artwork, music, sports, metaverse, or even selfies—are gaining traction in the digital sphere. They provide new ways for artists to generate money from their work, as well as a method for purchasers to support artists and, well, have the bragging rights of having unique material. However, they have faced criticism for their environmental impact.

NFTs, you see, are typically housed on blockchain platforms or traded using bitcoin, both of which are known to be massive energy consumers. How? We'll explain in more detail later, but in summary, it's because it takes a lot of computer power to get the entire NFT ecosystem up and running.

Some feel that there are ways of reducing the environmental consequences of NFTs. Beeple, a $69 million NFT artist, has stated interest in creating his work carbon neutral or perhaps even carbon zero. In an official statement, he said that he can accomplish this by renewable power, conservation initiatives, or technology that removes carbon from the environment to balance the emissions from the trading or minting of NFTs.

But what precisely is the environmental impact of NFTs? Is there something that could be done in order to fix, or improve this problem? Let us explain the environmental impact of NFTs, and blockchain technology first, and then, we will shift to the possible ways of solving the problem.

NFTs require a lot of energy - Why?

The major reason NFTs consume so much

energy is since they are stored on blockchain platforms. Since blockchain is a book of data that everyone can read, then individuals must validate those records as well.

This is when miners enter the picture. Miners are the auditors of blockchain systems, competing with their computers or "rigs" to authenticate transactions in return for tokens and incentives. According to Matthew Azada, a crypto trader and investor, it's similar to a game in which the platform provides a riddle for miners to decrypt and then picks a proper solution at random. This form of agreement is known as "proof-of-work."

Because miners compete for prizes (typically in the form of cryptocurrencies such as Ethereum and Bitcoin), they sometimes combine their efforts to boost their chances of getting chosen—sort of like a lottery.

There have been several preliminary calculations of how much electricity an NFT consumes and, as a result, how much solar system pollution it produces.

Take, for example, Space Cat, an NFT that is just a GIF showing a cat in a rocket traveling to the moon. Per the website cryptoart.wtf, Space Cat's carbon footprint is comparable to a two-month supply of power for an EU inhabitant. That website used to allow users to browse the projected greenhouse gas emissions connected with particular NFTs until its author, Memo Akten, removed it on March 12th.

Akten, a digital artist, examined 18,000 NFTs and discovered that the average NFT had a carbon footprint that is somewhat smaller than Space Cat's but still equal to more than a month's worth of power for an EU resident.

Because the crypto art trend is still relatively new, none of the data available has been examined by other specialists. Ethereum, like other major cryptocurrencies, is based on a technique known as "proof of work," which consumes a lot of energy. Performing a payment on Ethereum incurs a cost, which is paradoxically referred to as "gas."

Because there is no third party, such as a bank, to supervise transactions, proof of work serves as a form of security method for cryptocurrencies such as Ethereum and Bitcoin. The method compels customers to solve hard riddles using energy-guzzling equipment in order to keep bank information secure. Solving the riddles allows users, or miners, to add a new "block" of validated transactions to the blockchain, a decentralized record.

As a reward, the miner receives fresh tokens or transaction fees. On purpose, the procedure is extremely inefficient in terms of energy use. The notion is that consuming excessive amounts of power — and most likely paying a high price for it — makes it less advantageous for someone to muck up the ledger. As a result, Ethereum consumes about the same amount of energy as the whole nation of Libya.

When someone creates, buys, or trades an NFT with Ethereum, they are accountable for a portion of the emissions produced by those miners. What remains to be seen is whether NFTs significantly increase Ethereum emissions or if they just assume responsibility for pollution that miners would have created anyhow. Miners would still be working on riddles and pollution if NFTs did not exist. Furthermore, NFTs account for a relatively modest proportion of total Ethereum transactions.

As per Joseph Pallant, founder of the organization Blockchain for Climate Foundation, determining the guilt of NFTs is similar to estimating your contribution of emissions from a commercial airline travel. (Wang, & Chen, 2021) You are definitely accountable for a percentage of the plane's emissions if you are on board. But even if you hadn't purchased the ticket, the jet would have gone off with other passengers and polluted the same amount.

Individual conduct, on the other hand, becomes a greater issue when it causes patterns. If enough individuals decide to start flying who weren't going to previously, an airline may opt to run additional flights, resulting in higher overall emissions.

"Many NFT transactions provide a larger economic signal to miners, which may lead to increasing emissions," Susanne Köhler, a PhD fellow at Denmark's Aalborg University who studies sustainable blockchain technology, wrote in an email

(Wang, & Chen, 2021). If NFTs drastically increase the value of Ethereum, miners may try to profit by increasing the number of devices they employ. In general, more machinery equals greater pollution.

Even if new computers are better at solving problems, making them increasingly energy-efficient, proof-of-work riddles are meant to become increasingly complex. Likewise, the system was meant to keep things as inefficient as possible.

An Eco-Friendly Path

At the COP26 summit in Scotland in April, 2022, world leaders clashed over actions to reduce carbon emissions. Meanwhile, in Canada, the oil-drilling capital, a tech business is doing everything in their power to initiate and promote carbon neutrality. Their main task - converting oil waste into ecologically friendly energy that fuels crypto mining

(Wang, & Chen, 2021). This self-sustaining technology, created by CurrencyWorks, will eventually help power the distribution of *Zero Contact*, a new film starring Anthony Hopkins that premiered in May 2022 as an NFT, without carbon footprint.

Municipalities in Canada pay a fee to dispose of their waste at the Canadian plant. That organic material—in this example, solid waste—is decomposed at high temperatures under pressure by a process known as pyrolysis. This creates electricity, which may be used for cryptocurrency mining; the plant can power up to 200 mining equipment by combining municipal and oilfield trash. With its massive oil tank and heavy metal pipes, the operation may appear to have nothing in common with the gleaming world of NFTs and Web3, the next era of virtual, and digital platforms and tools. However, with or without the guidelines of government leaders and their campaign promises, this industrial facility is playing an important role in the global energy revolution.

The factory in Edmonton, Alberta, is part of a growing movement in the cryptocurrency world to address the environmental effect of "mine" cryptocurrencies, a practice that has sparked global outrage due to its high energy consumption. According to one Cambridge University study, global bitcoin mining uses up more energy each year than Argentina as a whole (Wang, & Chen, 2021). At the beginning of the NFT rise, when NFT sales of mixed works of art and collectible goods totaled billions of dollars in trading volume.

Some may find it difficult to comprehend how a digital transaction—an exchange of binary codes shown in a sequence of flashing lights—can have such a profound influence on climate change. It's useful to keep in mind that every digital process uses energy. Per a NASDAQ research report, the worldwide banking industry utilizes around 263.72 Terawatt hours of energy every year (Wang, & Chen, 2021). Bitcoin consumes slightly less than half that amount. Mining for blockchain blocks is labor-intensive and hence energy-intensive by design.

But, not everything is bad. The crypto industry is trying to get past this problem and wants to evolve. A lot of platforms at the moment change their views and start to promote a healthy environment. Processes like those used at the Canadian facility, which employ a CurrencyWorks protocol called Zer00, are gaining momentum. Cryptocurrency information storage innovations provide appealing options. There are companies which are picky regarding the locations of mining coins, this is a fact.

However, crypto is still in its infancy, and each month introduces new efficiencies. Eli Ben-Sasson together with Uri Kolodny, engineers from Israel, and at the same time co-founders of the business StarkWare, are keen to emphasize the industry's fast transformation. (Wang, & Chen, 2021) It's the Boomers in this environment, not the young programmers and Gen Z artists that get all the attention. Both have theoretical and intellectual roots.

They are, however, one of several groups who have discovered a method to lower the carbon footprint of Ethereum mining and transactions by stuffing more information into each block of the blockchain. Brands seeking to enter the NFT space, such as Marvel and Disney, have already agreed to use StarkWare's technology in their NFT launches, since Ethereum is presently the leader in NFT trading volume. (Wang, & Chen, 2021) And they just secured a $50 million Series C investment round at a valuation of $2 billion. According to StarkWare, their technique cuts energy usage by 200 to 200,000 times that of other solutions, but on a purely theoretical level, that figure is endless.

"If you think of each piece of a blockchain as something that emits a lot of CO2 because of all the mining that happens on, there are fixed costs that are very, really high," Ben-Sasson argued. (Wang, & Chen, 2021)

"Imagine it as an airplane that puts out a lot of carbon. However, if instead of 100 people on a flight, you could put 600,000 people on an airliner, then even though the airplane still emits the same amount of carbon—which is bad—the footprint per person is really rather good. And that is where we come in."

According to Kolodny, the company's technology can now put "more than a million" NFTs in a single block. (Wang, & Chen, 2021) StarkWare has created a tool known as a ZK which is also known as "zero knowledge" rollup that transfers transactions offchain, reducing energy consumption. It is an alternative to the basic proof of work technical contract upon which the blockchain is based.

This is one of the most contentious issues in the blockchain world right now: whether new chains that are not proof of work, as well as extra roll ups like StarkWare's, can—or will—be acceptable alternatives to bitcoin's basic "work." While Bitcoin and Ethereum continue to be proof of work, other rivals, such as Binance, Solana, Tezos, and Flow, are the more energy-light proof of stake and, hence, intrinsically more efficient. StarkWare is one form of a firm that provides a mechanism to make Ethereum transfers more efficient in their current state; it is noteworthy for its high-profile clientele.

The CEO of Immutable X, Robbie Ferguson, a firm that enables NFT transactions and claims to be carbon neutral, has been incorporating StarkWare's technology into its platform. He believes that a shift toward more environmentally friendly options in the crypto realm is unavoidable, both commercially and socially. (Wang, & Chen, 2021)

"I don't believe the crypto space is that concerned," he said. "I believe the crypto sector is on a mission to reduce financial middlemen while simultaneously promoting digital ownership. I believe that is the most important mission for the majority of them. However, mainstream enterprises and, without a doubt, mainstream consumers [care]. It's also something we're quite passionate about." (Wang, & Chen, 2021) When huge brands and corporations demand that carbon neutrality be embedded into their work, Ferguson says NFT networks and blockchain activities like his have no choice but to think about how to make that happen.

According to Cameron Chell, CEO of CurrencyWorks, the company that operates the Canadian plant, all new solutions for tidying up crypto have a place in the technology's future; it's one of the main topics that comes up in "every conversation" about the environmental perspective of crypto and NFT creation. (Wang, & Chen, 2021) "It's a huge X against your project if it doesn't have a larger good effect, if it doesn't speak to the community, and if it has a major carbon footprint," he adds. In the near future, he envisions his own organization becoming completely self-sufficient on recycled energy. Others would have to forge their own paths to that end. However, as the industry grows—over $330 million in NFT sales - it will compel acceptance, according to executives like Chell and technologists like Kolodny and Ben-Sasson who are ecstatic about their possibilities.

Ethereum Alternatives

There are other methods for making a blockchain safe that are less harmful to the environment. A mechanism known as "proof of stake" is the most popular solution to proof of work.

NBA's Top Shot, a market where sports fans can purchase NBA highlights as NFTs, runs on the Flow blockchain, which is an example of a more centralized blockchain that uses the proof-of-stake architecture. To deter negative conduct, this system still requires players to have some form of skin in the game. Instead of having to pay for massive quantities of power to enter the game, players must instead "stake" some of their very own cryptocurrency tokens in the system to "show" they have a "stake" in maintaining the ledger correctly. (Wang, & Chen, 2021) If they are detected doing something illegal, they will be punished by losing those tokens. This eliminates the need for computers to answer complicated riddles, hence eliminating emissions.

For years, Ethereum has stated that it will ultimately transition to proof of stake. Optimists in crypto art are aiming for this. That would effectively mean that Ethereum's power use would plummet to nearly nil over the course of a day or overnight.

The issue is that many have been waiting for Ethereum to make the adjustment for years, and others are doubtful that it would ever do so. First, Ethereum must persuade everyone that the authentication process is the way to go. Otherwise, the entire system may fail.

"If not, everyone cooperates with that adjustment, the network will come apart," warned economist Alex de Vries. "If everyone isn't using the same program, it can literally split into numerous chains." That is the disadvantage of attempting to update public blockchains such as Ethereum." (Wang, & Chen, 2021)

Private blockchains also exist, and some, such as Flow, are entirely dedicated to NFT transactions, enabling them to avoid some of the challenges associated with cryptocurrencies such as Ethereum. However, these blockchains deviate from the original purpose of cryptocurrencies, which was to build a decentralized network where anybody may conduct transactions without the control of a single entity.

There are various techniques to reduce NFT emissions while maintaining a more decentralized proof-of-work network. (Wang, & Chen, 2021) One possible approach is to add another "layer" to the present blockchain. Working on this second layer can help conserve energy since transactions take place "off-chain," away from the electricity proof-of-work mechanism. For example, two individuals who wish to trade NFTs may create their own "channel" on the second tier where they could conduct an almost infinite number of transactions. They may settle up the net outcome of their transactions back on the blockchain where it can be put to the verified database via the proof-of-work procedure once they're done conducting business. (Wang, & Chen, 2021)

Art NFTs aren't only a trend for a subset of people. Furthermore, this technological innovation is challenging and has already established concepts of art and lowering barriers for people who wish to engage via creation or collection.

Chapter 3: Impact on NFTs on the Environment

A rt NFTs are not a trend for people. This technological innovation is challenging, and has already established concepts of art. It has also been lowering barriers for people who wish to engage in creativity via creation of many art collections.

A Critical Feature for the Future of Art

We've demonstrated that they're non-fungible, which enables an artist to mint an easily repeatable digital item, like as an image or a movie, to create a one-of-a-kind digital object.

This indicates a spot of origin and serves as a form of validity certificate. When NFT is purchased, the transaction is publicly registered and archived via blockchain technology, producing a record that can be traced back to the creator eternally. (Brooks,

2021) This is referred to as origin in the art world. It is one method of determining the validity of an artifact.

By providing technology capable of establishing originality and credibility to an otherwise endlessly replicable product, you are basically reintroducing the entire notion of originality to a digital realm swamped in duplicates. In addition, by attaching that digital thing to its creator , you reinforce authorship. (Brooks, 2021)

This means that the artist can keep his or her authorship while engaging in a digital art market. The picture can be saved by right-clicking it, but the NFT cannot be saved by right-clicking it. That is still on the blockchain. (Brooks, 2021)

The secondary market is a significant advantage of NFTs over the traditional art market. (Brooks, 2021) Each time an NFT is resold, the artist receives a share of the proceeds. This solves an issue that has always persisted in the art world: purchasing immediately from artists while they are still undiscovered, then selling that work for ten times more the original value. When this occurs, collectors become wealthier, but artists do not. The artist is compensated for each resale of their work through NFTs.

Anil Dash, an entrepreneur described this in the perfect way possible with an example. Namely, he recalls collaborating with Kevin McCoy to develop "the very first blockchain-backed method of demonstrating ownership through an original digital work." He saw it as a method for creators to retake control of their work, which was and is badly needed, and he added: "Our idea of enabling artists hasn't yet actually happened, but it has produced a lot of financially marketable excitement."

NFTs have produced a massive amount of economically exploitable buzz. But what about the part about supporting creators? That is also occurring. Both of these statements are correct.

Yatreda is an Ethiopian art collective. The work, headed by Kiya Tadele, reconstructs the past through breathtaking motion images of key historical individuals.

Those photographs, presented in a style evocative of 19th century photographs, have the capacity to bring history to life. The artwork has a lovely, mesmerizing pace.

Tadele outlines the series' motive in a discussion:

"We could be considered as a patriotic nation, but, without doubt, there are some things missing. We examine all of the great famous movies, sculptures, and artwork created by other countries

based on their tales. "Why doesn't a person do anything like this for Ethiopia?" one wonders. So, who exactly would be that someone? We concluded that someone could be us."

The "we" in the previous sentence are Kita Tadele, with her sisters Suzy and Roman Tadele, her fiancé Joey Lawrence, and friends Abiy and Tigist.

Roman does extensive history research — what weapons were used, what individuals wore and looked like at the period. Suzy, the other sister, can use her machine to adapt garments or construct anything from scratch. So everything they can't find in a gallery or antique shops, they can manufacture. Joey is the lighting wizard who can handle every technical aspect. In the editing software, Tadele handles the camera, leads the actors, and selects the final video choice for the NFT.

Every team member brings "in the same way as bones in the human in a skeleton do. Each person has a distinct and vital function." Giving expression to the past has a tremendous amount of power. Leaders and affluent patrons have a long history of purchasing art to maintain their own legacies, leaving artists with a visual history that overwhelmingly represents those with the most money and power. Yatreda contributes to this tradition by rewriting their own history on their own.

They also have a series called *Movement of the Ancestors*, which makes excellent use of the digital media. They achieve this by creating and documenting traditional dance and music performances at the same time. These cinematic loops are exciting and fascinating.

We would like to highlight how Tadele discusses her decision to mint Yatreda's artwork as

NFTs:

"I used to work extremely hard as a model or on the stages of other shooters or films, but we would send our work to the internet or to a customer. I had a major question running through my head: Do I own what I develop? I've always wanted to be my own person. With NFTs, I was able to construct my own idea and show it to the world — and, most significantly, I was able to do something traditional that kept my dignity. It became significant, similar to going to a museum or an art exhibit."

That's it. The reason why NFTs are so essential in the arts. They reestablish the artist's power at a time when the choices are to create commercial work for companies or to dump art into the black abyss of social media sites. Yatreda may make art on their own terms, retain their ownership as artists, and be compensated for their work without the need for established galleries or businesses. And if their work is bought, they will continue to receive a share of each sale, guaranteeing that if the value of their art rises, they will gain.

Yatreda's art has sold at prices similar to a big gallery event in London but without the production, traveling, or gallery fee. They may continue to work in Ethiopia because of their worldwide connectedness. (Brooks, 2021)

The decentralization of cryptocurrency is well-known. In reality, NFTs have the ability to decentralize the art world by removing global borders and making this market available to people who have hitherto been excluded. (Brooks, 2021)

After all, the most valuable auction for a work of art by a living artist occurred in 2021, behind just Jeff Koons and David Hockney—and it was for a piece that exists only as a JPEG format. Namely, Beeple's

sold for $69.3 million. Indeed, Beeple started a new

era for the art world. It proved that anything is

possible, and that the artists could shift the game to

their benefit.

Chapter 4:   NFTs and The Future of Arts

For a long period of time, it was thought that the blockchain technology has been nothing more than a payment network. And that it is with tight ties to financial use cases. Nevertheless, NFTs have altered this. We can confidently claim that the blockchain is now comparable to one enormous, decentralized technology platform, encompassing a swath of diverse assets and dApps, complete with brands, cultures, and societies that give both economic and subjective social value.

NFTs also provide a new paradigm in how we capture physical assets and treat purely digital goods. As the world continues to digitalize, the demand for technology that can securely verify digital assets will only increase. NFTs fill this need and have the ability to revolutionize the way we operate as a community.

There are several NFT applications, ranging from art to gaming. Verifying provenance is a frequent use case, but we are still only exploring the possibilities.

Any service or product that is or depends on an intermediate can be tokenized using an NFT. Important papers such as legally binding contracts, home deeds, policies, and licenses are prime candidates for the future. NFTs will accomplish the same for the digital economy that property rights did for previous economies.

And if enterprises and governments do not engage in the decentralized system, the technology underpinning NFTs is too important to ignore. At least they would have to evaluate the consequences of how NFTs may drastically cut layers of bureaucracy.

The Current Possibilities

So far, NFTs have mostly been used as a proof of authenticity for digital artwork. However, their applications are fast evolving—today, they may verify ownership and provide exclusive access to VIP privileges, unique material, and asset rights. Ten examples of alternate uses for NFTs are shown below, varying from blockchain real estate rights to transferable marketing advantages.

Location-Based NFTs

The main concept behind NFTs is that their token records can include geolocation metadata from gadgets or other inputs. This implies that the NFT can refer to a specific item in real space or just to a place.

The location based NFT concept is now being tested for NFT gaming. Zombie Inu is such an initiative, with its ZINU coin gaining traction. Its primary use is in 3D augmented reality, with geolocation capabilities on the way.

Kryptomon, the NFT-based site play to earn game, is one contest that combines all of these qualities. Kryptomon blends the metaverse idea of competing characters with unique location-tied personalities and treasure quests.

The metaverse is a system of three-dimensional virtual environments focusing on social interaction. It is frequently portrayed in futuristic and science fiction as a potential iteration online as a single, worldwide virtual environment that is aided by the usage of augmented and virtual reality headsets.

It is currently too early to demonstrate all location based NFT projects since they are not available yet. The competition for available space and the market for collectors will reflect the degree of demand. There is very little information available on the increased value of location based NFTs and it is unclear if they will change the game completely or will be something that is already seen or experienced.

Restaurant NFTs

Gary Vaynerchuk is changing the NFT restaurant game completely. Namely, he is allowing tastes to participate as well. The businessman is constructing a restaurant in which ownership of his business NFT is essential before dining. The NFT, which will open in 2022, will provide clients with access to the restaurant, which will have a cocktail bar as well as a private culinary event.

Vaynerchuk isn't the only restaurateur dabbling in digital treats. Marcus Samuelsson, a celebrity chef, is also looking at the possibilities that NFTs bring to his business. He produced an NFT that can be claimed for a special supper for four, followed by a work of art that ingeniously represents the chef's fried chicken. Samuelsson, like many other chefs, wishes to guarantee that the cooking arts are not forgotten in the new, digital world.

Marketing and Brand Perks

To specifically target messages for certain groups, marketers might generate tokens that are personalized to specific audiences. The idea of employing NFT advertising to retain its customers is that it allows their supporters to acquire one-of-a-kind, branded digital things – a definite method to secure a place in their fans' affections.

NFT DNA

Many genetics testing organizations have come under fire for their data privacy practices involving their customers' personal information. 23andMe, for example, was chastised for reselling aggregated data from their users. Nebula Genomics, on the other hand, wants to demonstrate that it values privacy. Nebula, created by Professor George Church, placed Church's DNA data in the system, where it will remain in perpetuity and cannot be deleted.

Church's DNA has significant historical relevance in the area of personal genomics. The NFT will be housed on the Ethereum blockchain, where it will contain the digital location of George's whole genetic data, which will be kept on a decentralized server.

NFT Tweets

Twitter, and tweets are also part of the trend of commercialized digital assets. Twitter co-founder

Jack Dorsey's first post on Twitter was sold for $2.9 million to a Malaysian businessman, or almost $100,000 per character. The proceeds go to the GiveDirectly Africa program. On March 15th, 2021, Elon Musk declared that he will sell a "song about NFTs as an NFT," which almost sold for a large price. The tweet was posted on v.cent, a website where consumers may purchase and trade blockchained tweets, before he formally published it. Before deciding to cancel the auction, he faced bids approximately close to $1 million.

Real Estate Title NFTs

NFTs can also be utilized to represent tangible things or real estate holdings. Fractional ownership is an illustration of this. By releasing tokens on the blockchain, landowners might sell a portion of their land to a huge number of small purchasers, or investors. Buyers might retain these tokens and earn an additional income, a profit divided on capital appreciation when they sell them, or both.

This might also enable consumers to acquire and sell partial ownership in investment homes in a liquid market without the use of a middleman. This would allow many more people to enter the world of real estate and provide better choices for those who need to release value without moving, or borrowing.

Clothing NFTs

NFTs have also made an appearance in the fashion industry—Uniswap socks, for example, are NFTs, present on the Ethereum blockchain, and they are exchanged like regular NFTs but can also be exchanged for an actual piece. Because these NFTs are linked to redeemable things, they trade at more fair prices. For now, these socks are estimated for

$100K.

The benefit of these NFTs is that the product is assured to be in excellent shape. Completely different from Jordan footwear, that always brings the chance of being worn. In this case, the owners of this NFT may exchange for unused socks with the confidence that what they can see is what they will receive. FTX, a cryptocurrency exchange, is also involved in redeemable clothes, with items such as redeemable condoms, or sweatpants.

Gaming NFTs

Buying stuff for an online game is not a novel concept; numerous games have offered products that can be purchased or sold for actual money on their interface. Runescape, for example, features in-game Gold that can be traded for around $10 for 100M gold. (Cliente, 2022) The "Dragon Lore" sniper skin in CS:GO costs $61,000. The only thing these things have in common is that they are managed by the centralized game server. Also, they both do not have access to the exact liquidity that is present on the blockchain.

"Play to earn" is the latest gaming concept promoted by crypto enthusiasts. Players may earn NFT products by playing games and selling them on markets at higher prices. These goods are frequently utilized to improve one's success in the game. Among the most notable examples of the idea is Axie Infinity, in which players may acquire a love potion that can be traded for 15 cents. (Cliente, 2022) Its popularity has skyrocketed in the Philippines, with individuals abandoning their jobs to pursue it.

Humans have historically assigned value to a wide range of objects, but with NFTs, we can now tokenize them. This opens up a slew of new prospects for the development of decentralized businesses and communities.

NFTs are not only changing the way we evaluate worth, but also the way we connect with one another. Take a glance at how the Loot NFT project evolved to observe how NFTs and decentralization have impacted the producer and creative economies. What we are experiencing is largely or entirely of tokenization into society, cultures, and even ourselves.

The digital world is here. It won't go anywhere as well. The NFTs are the entry point to digital ownership. Some may claim that we are on the verge of a digital apocalypse, but we are sure that practically everything will ultimately be tokenized.

Chapter 5: NFT Crash, If or When?

NFTs have expanded at an alarmingly rapid rate in recent years. As an NFT enthusiast, you are aware of how they are changing the way we experience our environment by linking our physical and virtual realities.

A lot of experts estimate that NFTs will eventually explode. They compare it to a real bubble. Though NFTs will ultimately crash, it is unknown when this will occur. The best guess is that it will be shortly.

People have found a way to add value to a lot of intangible things with the help of crypto, and NFTs. It is inevitable to say that they bring financial gain, in crypto, and physically. But, what happens if they crash? Most importantly, when will this happen?

Colborn Bell, a former investment banker, is

the first on the list that started warning people about NFTs crash. (Storey, 2022) Bell began collecting NFTs back in 2020 and has already built a sizable collection. He also established the Museum of Crypto Art, a virtual reality art exhibition facility.

Despite having a personal stake in the development of NFTs, Bell recently told the public that he is "prepared, I believe, for a devastating market meltdown." It's a fascinating and completely honest inside look as to what the NFT mania has become - and where it might be heading.

There are several possibilities that might lead to the NFT market collapsing. Among them are the following:

- Infinite supply
- Scams and copyright infringements
- Silent, bitcoin and other crypto crashes

- Changes in macroeconomic conditions

NFTs provide copyright of a digital asset but they are not powerful enough to stop other people from utilizing digital copies of that item. One of the reasons rich investors are willing to spend a lot of money on conventional physical artworks by van Gogh, Rembrandt or Monet is because the quantity of artworks is limited; the artists are long deceased and cannot create new paintings. NFT duplicates, unlike the real art, are prone to duplicates. This could become a serious problem one day.

Furthermore, since everything is digital, there is no discernible difference in look between an authentic JPEG file purchased for $69.3 million and a free online copy. (Storey, 2022) In principle, there is an endless supply of legally usable copies of NFTs, possibly exceeding demand and forcing prices to drop.

Since the blockchain cannot contain the real underlying digital asset, anybody purchasing an NFT is purchasing a link to the electronic artwork rather than the artwork itself. Despite the fact that buyers acquire rights to the link, the transaction costs associated with monitoring the limitless internet venues for displaying NFTs, detecting illicit usage, and investigating and punishing violations make it practically difficult to enforce the copyrights or discourage abuse. This severely restricts the asset's commercialization.

Since we have severe copyright regulations in place, NFTs' copyright breaches must be considered before investing. Prior to actually making an investment or purchasing something, as an investor or customer, you should investigate the IP (intellectual property ownership).

If one person incorporates some other

person's work into their work without possessing the rights to that piece, they, as well as any customers who did not conduct their thorough research, can be penalized. Infringement of copyright can lead an NFT to fall since high pricing and strong interest are unexpectedly unpleasant.

NFT frauds are a type of copyright violation. Nevertheless, a person may be unaware of a copyright violation, in which scammers take non-fungible tokens and resell them as one of their own for a percentage of the original price.

As these frauds spread, investors must conduct due diligence and ensure they are purchasing from a recognized seller who has a blue ticket. (Storey, 2022) Investigate the NFT that piques your curiosity.

Another concern is that NFTs are being created and sold alongside emerging technologies such as cryptocurrencies, or blockchain. There are presently several rival standards for generating, safeguarding, distributing, and certifying NFTs, such ERC-998, ERC-721, ERC-1155, non-flow, including flow standards, including Tezos' FA2. The consequent ambiguity about how ownership verification would be assured in perpetuity jeopardizes asset value and perhaps ownership.

Indeed, if the next generation of more advanced technology that surpasses crypto or blockchain is irreconcilable with safe NFT possession, the worth of NFTs may vanish. Companies dealing in NFTs now may not exist tomorrow, trying to muddy ownership rights.

The market volatility of the cryptocurrency that supports the NFT market is also a critical concern. NFT prices typically change in lockstep with cryptocurrency prices. When the cryptocurrency market crashed in 2018, so did the fledgling market for NFTs.

The mentality of purchasing luxury products will almost certainly put even more pressure on NFT rates. Most luxury items are so-called Veblen objects, having little value other than allowing owners to flaunt their money. As a result, they frequently earn substantial gains for sellers.

Changes in macroeconomic conditions may have a detrimental impact on the pricing of investment options such as NFTs and conventional artworks. Over the last two decades, the amount of billionaires in the globe has grown over fivefold, and accessible money ready to be placed in different asset classes has risen as a result. So yet, the Covid-19 crisis has just strengthened this tendency. (Schmedders, 2022) Much of the massive economic stimulus supplied by central banks flowed into financial markets, increasing the super-net rich's wealth even higher.

However, investor interest might be transitory. Following the global financial crisis of 2008, sales of artwork and other luxury goods fell by about 40%. (Schmedders, 2022) With central banks beginning to restrict monetary and fiscal policy in an effort to control inflation, new and experimental asset classes are likely to be penalized more severely than more dependable ones. (Schmedders, 2022) And the very volatile NFT market, which is based on digital currency with no backing, is far from a safe haven.

NFT prices will likely fall precipitously and permanently. They are still high for the time being and may continue to rise in the upcoming future, but the fall will come. (Schmedders, 2022) Investors who believe they can time the market are open to giving it a go, but their confidence is likely to be mistaken.

Conclusion

Would you like to dive into the vast and magnificent world of Non-Fungible Tokens, and discover not only the primary principle behind these, but also how they may be developed and how they connect to Blockchain technology? Do you want to create your personal digital art and learn new techniques? If this is your debut with non-Fungible tokens, don't be concerned.

This book contains all you need to know about NFTs. They are digital assets that contain specific details in their smart contracts. Because of this information, each NFT is distinct, and as a consequence, they cannot be quickly substituted by another token. Since no two NFTs are the same, they cannot be traded.

NFTs are a distinct type of investment since

they function as a type of token that may symbolize both physical and digital ownership of assets. NFTs, as bitcoin, may be bought and sold online and are effectively non-transferable goods. They are one-of-a-kind assets in every aspect. The price of NFTs is rising as they become more common. As a consequence, NFT innovators are making a lot of money.

But, before making any choice, always ensure that you own the copyrights to the thing you want to turn into an NFT. If you make an NFT for a digital asset that you do not own, you may face legal consequences.

Because of its deep ties to the actual world, it's also a wonderful way to promote crypto before others. NFTs, which vary from basketball trade cards to cute toys, allows a broader spectrum of people to engage in the bitcoin world.

NFTs are here to stay and will soon become the planet's next great thing. This is the ideal moment to begin your adventure. Be one of those people who can say, "I'm glad I engaged in this task."

Printed in the USA
CPSIA information can be obtained
at www.ICGtesting.com
LVHW021708190923
758613LV00005B/208